The Other Side of the Hill

The Other Side of the Hill

Celebrating Our Later Years

Antonia Albany

Santa Rosa, California

Albany Books
2777 Yulupa Avenue, #333
Santa Rosa, California 95405-8584

Printed in the United States of America
Published September 2015

Library of Congress Control Number:
ISBN:. 978-0-9966424-1-5

Design by Randall Friesen

This book is dedicated to my sister, Christine.

She never got to enjoy many of her senior years.
I miss her and wish we were sharing this prime time together.

Acknowledgments

For the past twenty years I have accumulated stories and written about the aging process from either my own perspective or the viewpoint of others. I would like to sincerely thank Randall Friesen for his expertise in editing and adapting this material, which appeared in various locations including my blog. He carefully turned my writings into something more readable and coherent. Tasks that were overwhelming to me were second nature for him.

Thanks also to my friend Norma Miller, and my husband, Rod Sverko, for reading and re-reading drafts and for providing invaluable input.

As always, I appreciate all my friends who continue

to inspire and who represent the graceful and grateful aging spoken of in these chapters.

Contents

Introduction

We have a choice. Every day when we swing our legs over the side of the bed and our feet touch the floor, we can decide how our day will be spent. Many of us at this age are retired or about to be. We have the entire day before us to do with as we wish.

Some of us turn on the TV or online games and plop ourselves down never to budge the entire day. Some of us engage with family and friends and seek out satisfying activities such as volunteer work, reading, writing, gardening, crafting or spending time in nature, alone or with friends.

It doesn't matter whether you are alone or coupled, whether you have unlimited financial resources or are on a limited budget. It doesn't matter where you live or how educated you are. There are always fun and entertaining things to do and ways to be in this world during your senior-dom that will create for a very satisfying latter part of your life.

This book shares some of what I have learned about aging and how I have created a fun and rewarding life through humor, spirituality, friendships, curiosity and trial and error. My hope is that you find yourself on some of the pages here and are able to take away something that will enrich your life.

These just might be the best years of your life!

The Other Side
of the Hill

The Art of Aging Gracefully

*"Whining is not only graceless, but it can be dangerous.
It can alert a brute that a victim is in the neighborhood."*
—*Maya Angelou*

I care about aging gracefully because I've found that I
have more fun when I approach everything with grace.
Coming from a place of grace gives me a strong sense
of gratitude and allows for the pause that refreshes, so
to speak. When I'm in grace, I'm not a "bull in a china
shop," never slowing down long enough to really enjoy the process. As I get older, the process needs to be

just as worthwhile as the end result. I want to have fun along the way. The end result then becomes the icing on the cake.

Perhaps it's best to define grace as what it isn't rather than what it is. Grace isn't about money, where you went to school, or friends in high places. It isn't about the car you drive or the clothes you wear. You can still live in grace even if you know nothing about wine, modern art or fine dining. Living a graceful life is all about attitude.

A graceful life is characterized by a foundation of gratitude. All things in my life spring forth from a strong sense of appreciation. I don't take for granted my freedom, my health, my friends or the ability to read and write. I am thankful to be surrounded by beautiful things.

To fully incorporate gratitude into my life I do the following every day:

- When I first awake and right before going to sleep, I acknowledge that my life is full and fun and that I am blessed with an abundance of love.
- I share the resources I have available to me, such as time, money, energy or knowledge.

An important trait in a graceful life is patience, and I've got to admit I'm still working on this one. Through patience one can truly allow all the senses to take in and digest that which surrounds us: the tastes, the sights and the sounds, whether we live in the heart of a bustling city or the quiet calm of the countryside. I like letting those influences slowly wash over my senses rather than being rudely slapped by them and then moving along. I want to luxuriate, savor and, ideally, share these feelings with others.

I focus on being gracefully patient in my senior years by:

- Taking the time to put the needs and desires of others ahead of my own, to assist others in achieving their goals before mine are realized
- Taking a pause before reacting in either positive or negative situations.

Grace used to be something I said before meals, and while it may still be that, it is so much more. Today I smell the flowers with a smile. I am able to laugh at myself and feel compassion for all my foibles. This is how grace shows up in my life today. Grace is accepting the way life is without complaint and writing a new personal history every day. Finally, grace is a softness, a comfort, a supportive gleam in my eye whether I'm trying to solve a problem or just enjoying the simplicity of my day.

I'm thrilled to have survived my youth unscathed. Does grace have a place in your life? What does it look like for you?

The Impact of
Social Media on Our Lives

I went through a period of time when I did a lot of moping around, lamenting about being the only member of my family of origin left and about not having any children of my own.

At that time, my spouse of twenty-four years had recently passed away, which obviously left me feeling alone and lonely. At this time I painted a fairly desolate picture of life as a senior citizen. Most of my friends, however, weren't buying it. They knew that I was plugged into a larger circle of friends who love and support me via social media such as Facebook and Twitter.

We seniors have witnessed an electronic revolution over the course of our lives. When we were in our single digits, we didn't have things such as electric garage door openers or remote TV controls, let alone the high speed information now available through personal computers.

Seniors these days are taking private, one-on-one instruction or classes at junior colleges and senior centers to learn the necessary skills to get and stay connected in this digital world. We understand that social media helps alleviate the isolation, loneliness and depression that may be brought on as family and friends move away and become less accessible, and as our mobility and independence begin to decline.

Social networking has created a new community for elders, especially those who are physically unable to leave their homes. Increasing numbers of older people are going online, and statistics from the Pew Research Center show that one-third of people over 65 used social networking sites in 2014, compared with six percent three years prior.

Once trained, most seniors easily and happily latch

onto social media. However, a significant segment of the older population expresses stress and anxiety about using it. Some seniors find it difficult to grasp the mechanics of navigating the computer itself, to say nothing of the intangible World Wide Web. In addition, having so much information available highlights just how much they don't know, and that can be depressing.

My life has been greatly enhanced by social media and the Internet. For those who may not be so comfortable learning about this new world, it is worthwhile to search out small group or one-on-one training sessions for elders. It is a terrific new way to acquire and maintain friendships. And if you're already up to speed, how can you help others who might benefit from this connection widen their world?

The Gift of Celebration

It's very simple. Nothing to research, nothing to buy.
Nothing to prepare, nothing to do. Nothing to cook
or wrap or save up for. Nothing to share, nothing to
worry about. It's free. It's a gift to yourself. Ready for
it? Here it is:

Celebrate.

That's it, just celebrate. Celebrate what, you ask?
Celebrate the breath that sustains you, that keeps
your whole being moving and growing and feeling.

Celebrate the simplicity of life and try laughing at yourself if you are making things more complicated than necessary.

Celebrate the diversity of people around the world that broadens our spectrum of color and experiences.

Celebrate how calm you instantly become when you close your eyes and sink into the loving arms of solitude.

Celebrate the color of the water on that special day last spring when you thought you had never seen a more sparkling periwinkle blue.

Celebrate the bounty that floats you through life, the abundance that surrounds you and brings you contentment.

Celebrate the wet nose poke of a pet seeking the touch of your love.

Celebrate the seasons with all their good and not so

good parts. They are the continuation of life and death.

Celebrate friendship, that soft place to fall, that place without envy, jealousy or upset.

Celebrate family, its imperfections and its purity, whether it's biological or created.

Celebrate spirit and the joy of *all* seasons.

Six Steps to Pump Up Your Life

1. Promise positive self-talk.

You can truly be your own worst enemy. No one can be more rigid and more unforgiving of your errors than you yourself. Have you ever said to a friend, "Gosh, you would never be as mean to me as you are to yourself."?

Having a negative attitude toward yourself is a habit. And like any habit, it can be broken. Make the commitment to catch yourself when you hear negative self-talk. Listen to recordings or pod casts with positive affirmations, such as those by Louise Hay. Tell others that you are trying to stop talking trash about yourself, and give yourself a huge pat on the back when you're successful.

2. Promise to practice patience with yourself and others.

As senior citizens it's more important than ever that we slow down to enjoy all that life has to offer. It's no longer the end result as much as it is the journey. We have nothing to prove about getting to the end of the race first. Today is the day to savor each part of the process.

Like self-talk, lack of patience is a habit, and this habit, too, can be broken through conscious attention and determination.

3. Promise to be less opinionated.

The difficult fact is, people don't really want your opinion unless they specifically ask for it. So in the meantime, zip it and be a good listener. Provide feedback only when asked, and let them know they've been heard.

4. Promise to be there for others.

One of the greatest gifts we have to share with others is ourselves—our time, our money, our support. But don't put the needs of others ahead of your own if, in doing so, you sacrifice your own well-being.

Being there for others requires tuning in to what's happening around you. Do you have friends or family who could benefit from having someone simply listen to them? Is there someone you know who would appreciate your support? Look around.

5. Promise to create or widen a spiritual connection.

What does Spirit mean to you? Only you can decide. Perhaps it's worshiping at a religious center. Perhaps it's a peaceful walk in nature. Whatever it is, your connection to Spirit will deeply enhance your life. It doesn't cost anything, it can be done at any time and in any place, and it can instantly make you feel better. Spiritual connection is like a warm cup of soup. Feel it spread throughout your body. It's a powerful tool.

6. Promise to lighten up.

Is every problem really such a big deal? Is your sense

of self compromised? Does it violate all you know to be right and true? If not, lighten up and let it go. There will always be something to make you feel uptight, angry, frustrated or resentful. You get to chose how you respond.

For each of these six promises to enhance your life, there are six million others. What are yours? Write them down and post them somewhere so you will be reminded daily of their power.

A Reflection of Myself

Self-image is one of those subjects I've always resisted writing about. I'm uncertain about what the smartest, most articulate way to approach it might be. What if I receive criticism for it? I've let this lack of perfection and fear of ridicule stop me from broaching the topic all together. No more.

During my formative years, my appearance represented the entirety of who I was. I was never satisfied with the way I looked. I never regarded appearance as merely one part of who I was; it completely defined me.

As I've matured and gotten older, both physically and

emotionally, the issue of appearance has faded into the background and been replaced by other more meaningful qualities. Or so I thought. It soon reared its ugly head when I found myself avoiding the idea of filming a video post.

What makes people feel attractive or unattractive? What makes us feel like keeping our eyes lowered or standing in the back of the room? For each one of us who feels insecure in our appearance, there are equal numbers of people like my friend Marilyn.

Marilyn is 5'10" and weighs 230. She is 60 years old and newly single. Throughout her life, Marilyn has held the attention of men and had a large group of loving female friends. Now that she is single again, she enjoys the company of smart, fun-loving men who appreciate the way she shows up in the world. What is the difference between her and me, who, when newly widowed nearly three years ago, found myself happy to close up shop, feeling myself greatly lacking in the looks department?

The difference is our belief systems. Marilyn believes in her attractiveness. She believes she possesses a variety of qualities to attract others. I don't know whether Marilyn sees a gorgeous woman when she looks in the mirror or if she has simply internalized the belief that attractiveness is not merely physical. It doesn't really matter, because she is comfortable with herself, and that shows through in any relationship.

My beliefs about my appearance were first created at home, where I was seen as an extension of my mother. My mom sent me to charm school so I would learn to mask any undesirable physical attributes. The second influence on how I felt about my appearance came from the media. No one doubts the overwhelmingly out-of-whack perception that results from our acceptance of the media's standard of beauty. If we are not otherwise enlightened, it becomes easy to believe those unrelenting messages. Over the years, I have accepted this negative input hook, line and sinker. And the message was loud and clear: You are not smart, articulate, witty or interesting unless you are attractive. Never mind how you feel inside or how developed your self-esteem is.

Have you ever based your worth on the way you looked? Or have you always felt secure in your appearance as merely one aspect of the wonderfulness of you? How do you feel about the way you look today?

I wish I could say I was well on my way to improving my beliefs, but I'm not completely there yet. I know that the following would help change my perspective:

- Realize that looks change. Look inside to see what you have in addition to your appearance.
- Understand that appearance is only one aspect of who you are.
- Expand the definition of appearance to include the outward parts as a reflection of the goodness within.
- Work with affirmations, such as, "My outside reflects the goodness and joy inside my heart and soul."

Childless Seniors Reflect

There are a couple of reasons why I never had children, but foremost was that it was difficult for me to conceive; I couldn't stay pregnant longer than a few days. While I wanted to have children and went so far as to have a couple of medical procedures to help the process along, in hindsight I was not overly disturbed that I was not able to have children during my child-bearing years. Many couples consciously choose a life without children.

As I've gotten older, the fact that I am childless has moved laterally into another separate issue: Who is going to take care of me as I age? Sound selfish? I don't think so. I think it's just good planning to consider possible options. I am well aware, however, that having children in no way guarantees an old age filled with built-in caretakers.

Our society would be strengthened by implementing more services to care for elders without family members in the picture. As reported at YaleGlobal Online, "In the U.S., based on the experiences of several states, childless older adults were likely to have higher medical costs and more complex health-care needs than older couples with children." All we have to do is look around to feel the anticipated substantial cutbacks and rejection of proposed entitlements that might provide funding and human resources to care for older adults who don't have children to help them as they age.

I recently conducted one of my highly unscientific polls with a few of my married or formerly-married friends who never had children in which I asked the following five questions:

1. Did you plan to not have children or did it just work out that way?

2. Did your spouse have children from a previous relationship, and, if so, did the children ever live with you? For how long? What were their genders and ages?

3. How do you think your life has been different without children than had you had children of your own?

4. Are you sad, happy, or neutral about not having had children?

5. What do you think you missed by not having had children?

In general, most of the women who responded took the fact of not having children in stride. Some didn't want them and some did. About half of the women, including myself, went on to have relationships with men who had children from previous marriages. Most of the women had satisfying relationships with those children, whether the children lived in the home with them or were already grown and lived elsewhere. As with any poll, there were women who offered wildly different responses than these generalities.

While most agreed their lives would have been vastly

different if they'd had children of their own, no one could state specifically what they thought those differences would have been. It would have been difficult for me to predict how things would have been different, too. The only thing that I feel I intentionally created in my life as a result of not having kids is a large circle of female friends. Perhaps we parent and act as siblings for each other.

The fourth question in my survey produced the most poignant answers. While a few of the women who consciously chose not to have children expressed happiness or neutrality about not having kids, most expressed sadness. It wasn't the kind of sadness that permeated a lifetime, but it was expressed as a sense of missing out on something wonderful. Some days were harder to handle than others. Personally, I will always wish I could see a child of mine graduate from school, get married and have children of their own. I will miss having a kid throw their arms around me and squeak, "I love you." I won't, however, miss having to pay for an education or wedding!

All the women I interviewed were coping just fine.

They had either created a family of friends, or treated their stepchildren as their own, or simply enjoyed a life of not having to share time, energy and resources with children who require buckets of attention. These women share their lives with their spouses, pets, hobbies, volunteer projects, and extended family and friends.

Like me, a few women expressed concern about not having children who could care for them as they enter old age. Generally I feel optimistic about the future of women who have no children of their own. It's good to see that we're not stuck in negative energy about being childless, but that we instead are making the most of our lives in whatever we do.

The question of what will happen to us as we age and need assistance will remain, but I know there are lots of options. Co-habitation, group homes, in-home care, and long term insurance may provide answers for many. In my case, I'm cultivating a large group of younger friends and also taking great care of myself now so as to not require special attention when I'm older. I'm grateful for an abundance of role models to show me the way.

The Other Side of the Hill

A Hole in My Heart

Heart sayings:

  ~ take a comment to heart

  ~ feeling a heart connection

  ~ a bleeding heart

  ~ a heart-to-heart

  ~ after my own heart

  ~ absence makes the heart grow fonder

  ~ have a change of heart

  ~ eat your heart out

  ~ a heart of stone; a heart of gold

  ~ coming from the heart

The preceding phrases don't refer to the physical heart that beats inside each of us, but rather to an emotional state that speaks to the intimate relationship between mind and body.

While the medical community may not put much stock in the strong connection between the physical and emotional, there are many spiritual students who do. And the number of people who adhere to this idea and accept the fact that our thoughts and emotions significantly affect our physical well-being is growing every day.

Whenever I have a problem or some situation that is causing me grief, I take it to heart. What this means is that I literally sit in silence, in meditation, and think of something positive, something that brings me joy. Usually I think about my cat, Kali. When I think of my love for her and the joy she brings, I visualize the heart inside my chest begin to open and expand. This gradually expanding heart contains all the love and joy I feel. When I'm filled with this joy, I take that problem, situation, or person and plunk it right down in the middle of my heart. My problem becomes enveloped in all that joy and love. But how does that help me?

With the problem resting in my heart, I begin to see it as an extension of myself. Then I am able to focus on creating compassion for the problem or person. Sometimes I see the cause of the problem, even if it's some less-than-great behavior on the part of the antagonist. I'm able to objectively observe the reasoning behind it, even if it resulted in pain for me. I don't have to be thrilled about it, but I stop being upset and traumatized.

The second thing that happens is that I am able to remove myself emotionally from the issue. It is put into perspective, and that usually lessens its importance in my full and wonderful life. Nothing has happened to change the facts, but I feel calmer and happier. And nothing can be better than that.

My heart, not my brain, creates the resolution to my problem, because my heart is the brain of my well-being. It's a powerful organ, not just for the love that is created by and radiates from it, but for its ability to address my problems. I can honestly say I have never solved problems more effectively.

The heart is a powerful tool. The love and positive feelings created by the heart spread throughout your being, and you are made better for it.

A *Mirepoix* of Spiritual Growth

One of the most significant comforts throughout my senior years has been my spiritual connection. As I have coped with aging and everything that comes with it, Spirit has been there with me, never preaching, just listening and reminding me that I am exactly where I'm supposed to be. I've cultivated what I consider to be the three main aspects of spiritual practice. I call it my *mirepoix* of spiritual growth.

Mirepoix is a French word meaning the combination of sautéed carrots, onions and celery which is the basis for thousands of tasty culinary dishes. It's a trifecta of flavors that supports and enhances the rest of the dish, just as meditation, exercise and connections with others is a trifecta of spiritual stability on which to grow and change. It is this spiritual *mirepoix* that keeps me focused, confident and strong enough to withstand anything thrown at me.

In the early 1970s I studied transcendental meditation through the Maharishi Mahesh Yogi Program in Berkeley, California. Since that time I've maintained a semi-regular meditating practice. I have found it to be a powerful tool in aligning where I am at any given time with where I want to be.

Meditation helps me focus, it helps me let go, and it helps me see what is important in my life. It grounds me and provides profound solace when the world around me seems topsy-turvy and chaotic. And it costs nothing! You need no formal training to meditate. You can find many good books on the subject, which will inform and guide you to a new level of spiritual growth.

Exercise is another essential component of spiritual growth. In no way do you have to be a triathlete in order to expand yourself spiritually. All I mean by "exercise" in this context is basic body movement. Time in front of the computer or TV is best balanced with walking, yoga or other physical activities. When you sit for long periods of time, your body feels heavier and it becomes more difficult to get your blood pumping. Moving things around stimulates the mind and soul as well as the body.

Active relationships are critical to any kind of growth, including spiritual. If I spend more than two days in isolation, either writing or just being apart from other people, I tend to spiral downward. Friends are a comfort, a soft place to fall, an anchor when the seas are choppy, and champions to encourage and applaud you. They are your colleagues in fun. Be a good friend to have a good friend. Friends are gold.

These are the main elements I use to continue to grow my spirituality. What is your recipe for expanding the comfort of spirit?

All Is Well

When I meditate, I use the phrase "All is well" as my mantra. This phrase carries significant power in calming me and helping me focus. I often repeat these three words at other times of day as well, not only during meditation.

When I am afraid and unsure about an outcome, I remember that all is well. When life swirls around me and I feel out of control, I remember that all is well. When I worry about nothing and everything, I remember that all is well. When I am discouraged and inconsolable, I remember that all is well.

Each time I successfully replace a negative attitude with one more positive, affirming that all is well, I take a step off the emotional roller coaster of life with all its ups and downs. Staying positive doesn't always solve the problem, but I do know that a negative attitude will never solve anything. Besides, "Fake it until you make it" has worked for me in the past. Sometimes you have to think it before you can live it.

"All is well" reminds me that I can quit trying to fix everything and everyone. It is a phrase which allows me to let go. I am reminded to live my best life and let others live theirs. I trust and believe in a Universe that provides for me.

These days, when something unpleasant happens, I look for the opportunity that is created in its wake. Getting laid-off can provide for a better job. A divorce or breakup can open space in your heart for a greater love. Challenging financial times can bring a huge sense of gratitude for the simple things in life. At the very least, an opportunity to learn from the experience is created.

Let "all is well" provide comfort in your life.

After You've Gone

Have you ever noticed how we talk about people while they're alive compared to how we talk about them after they've passed away? It's usually very different.

While someone is alive, we might speak glowingly of them by acknowledging their achievements: "Jim has risen to the level of president of the company only ten years after entering the corporation at the mail-room level," or "Janice has been able to bring in to her non-profit organization nearly triple the funds of her predecessor."

Once that person is gone, however, the things that we

consider to be a person's noteworthy successes change. They become, "Jim generously opened his home every year to at-risk youth and provided mentoring opportunities to help inner city kids get ahead in school," and "Janice was known for her compassion and enthusiasm. She gave her time, money, and talents so local senior groups could participate in the arts that might not otherwise be available to them."

Doesn't it look like one might be part of a resumé and the other part of a eulogy? Which one is more important? I'm not sure one is more important than another, but I am sure that when all is said and done I'd prefer that my name be followed by the eulogy rather than the resumé. Knowing the difference between the two can be valuable information.

We senior citizens are for the most part finished with work. We have achieved some things and didn't achieve others. We've spent time building a resumé of accolades. Do you think, however, that when someone hears your name after you're gone they'll remember and be impressed by the fact that you only missed two days of work in your 40 year career? I doubt it.

My point is to remind you that you can never spend too much time and effort developing those talents that will rarely show up on a resumé, like compassion, gentleness, patience, courage, truthfulness, loving-kindness, and the ability to make others laugh. Aren't you glad you already know how to be all these things?

Now go out and share these skills with others. Don't wait for the eulogy!

What Are Your Intentions?

"A gift consists not in what is done or given,
but in the intention of the giver or doer."
—*Seneca,* Moral Essays, Volume III: de Beneficiis

Everything you do begins with intention. Without intention you're just along for the ride, like a leaf floating on a puff of wind. With intention, you are able to create anything you want. Intention is one of the cornerstones of your most powerful self.

Have you ever started down a path to accomplish something and then felt that somewhere along the line you got off track and things became muddled, unclear and overwhelming? For me, it's not *if* but *how often.* A close look at your intentions can clear away any fog and confusion. I often write down my intention and post it on the bulletin board above my desk, where the list becomes the constant focus of my attention.

Having a clear intention keeps you on track toward your end result. Let's say you want a new car. You save money with the intention of having a safer and more reliable vehicle to transport your family around town. When you get to the dealer, however, that spiffy two-seater sports car beckons like a piece of chocolate cake, and the salesperson steers you toward the more expensive and less practical. If you're not clear on your intention, you may end up driving out with a vehicle that doesn't meet your needs. It's fun, but not what you set out to get.

We all have wants, and we want to get things our way. There is nothing wrong with wanting things, whether they are material possessions or emotional tranquility. The reason behind our wanting is more important. Do we want to spend thousands on improving our appearance to feel better about ourselves or to compete with a younger crowd? Staying focused on intentions can save lots of money.

Once an intention surfaces, it's effective to assess the thoughts and activities that will bring it to fruition. It's not a test. If your eyes aren't glued to your purpose all the time, life will not stop in its tracks. My purpose here is only to remind us all of what we know to be true.

A clear intention brings a brightness and clarity that can overcome uncertainly and confusion.

There's an App for That

When I'm not sure how to get where I want to go, I log on to MapQuest or Google Earth to find the location, and I'm soon given step-by-step directions how to get there: go 0.3 mi and turn left on Happiness Street; at the next stoplight bear right as the road forks at Memory Lane; your destination is on the left. Pretty nifty, even if the directions aren't always the most direct route.

When I run out of resources in my wallet, I log on to my bank's Web site and move my money around so I can make it until payday. When I don't know how to spell a word or when I need to find a store that sells little umbrellas for cocktails at my next patio party, I ask my loyal computer for a clue.

When I have a medical question or need to find out how physically healthy I am, I send a quick e-mail to my doctor and she gets back to me within a couple of hours, even if it's ten o'clock at night. When I crave a hit of spirituality I receive an injection by watching my minister's online videos or reading his informative and touching blog posts. So why can't I do the same with my emotional life?

Real life and the work involved require authentic participation, actual touching, face-to-face interaction, and problem solving in the presence of others. It can be pretty difficult to celebrate all that life has to offer with only a cold computer sitting in front of you, even one with a talented program that simulates real life events. Isn't there an app for that?

When I can't be in the room to see my girlfriend's new baby or on the field to watch my great nephew sprinting ahead of the pack at his track meet, the computer and social media certainly can fill in the blanks, but I do miss a great deal of the actual experience. I don't see the sweat of his labor as my nephew actually crossed the finish line, and he doesn't get to see me smiling and cheering his achievement. The limitations are obvious.

Yet when I'm frustrated or need insight on relationships or events, I want a quick answer. I admit it, I've Googled "How to be a better friend" and "How to express disappointment without getting angry." I've also looked up my role models, such as Ernest Holmes or Emma Curtis Hopkins, to see what they have to say about my spiritual issues. I've come to rely on my computer for many things, but solving real-people problems can't be entirely accomplished with an Internet connection.

I can't applaud my computer enough when it comes to teaching me what to do when my neighbor delivers a freshly caught, very much alive and kicking Dungeness crab to my door. ("Pop it in the freezer to put it to sleep.")

Access to all the information you'll ever need is handy, but it's not the complete solution to what ails us. I sometimes wonder if I'm missing out on people-to-people interactions because I use my digital devices too much. Admittedly, I've sometimes chosen those forms of communication over the face-to-face kind because I knew I could edit what I say before blathering forth.

If I didn't have my connection to all the information on the Internet, what would I do? I would keep trying to improve my interpersonal relationships. I would, though, have to call someone who could tell me how to handle a live crab. I would have to call my doctor's office for medical information, and I'd have to actually go out and connect with people in person, which wouldn't be so bad. I might flounder a bit more and make bigger mistakes, but I make pretty big ones now even with Wifi!

Some of my friends will scoff and say, "See, I told you I could live my life just fine without learning how to work one of them thar computer thingies." (They don't really talk like that!) I have mixed feelings. While their lives are lived in the purest connection of reaching out and connecting with other people, isn't it limited extensively by time, energy, money and availability?

Recently my computer experienced some major

problems. It involved the mouse and cursor having wildly divergent ideas about where to go on the screen, neither of which was governed by my participation. The problem was costly and inconvenient, and during the protracted correcting sessions I became more involved in my technician's personal life than I wanted to be. During this period of downtime I was able to reflect about the difference between mechanical problems versus people problems.

One of the best things to occur as a result of this computer problem was reading the book *Patience: The Art of Peaceful Living* by Allan Lokos. After devouring it, I'm sure that what I learned will help me with both computer problems and the foibles of living with and loving real, live humans.

I'm nowhere near abandoning my computer, but I feel a stronger sense of being able to handle things when it goes on the blink.

Can You Teach an Old Dog New Tricks?

I am not a big fan of change. As a Californian, I feel about change the same as I feel about earthquakes: I get irritated when things are exactly where I want them, and suddenly everything changes!

I resented the changes that came too quickly and unexpectedly in my senior years. I thought that after I retired, got my house the way I wanted it and organized my finances, everything would stay that way. Then came the financial crash of 2008. I was newly retired after working for forty years. Millions of people, me included, could do little but try to keep our heads above water as we watched our savings dwindle. Homes and jobs were lost, along with the general quality of our lives. With nothing left to do, I finally had to concede that change happens and that it's going to keep happening for the rest of my life.

Some change happens to us through no conscious action on our part, and some change we deliberately choose. When I chose to live apart from my spouse, I knew things would change, but I was open to that change because I thought it would strengthen my relationship with him, which it did. It's the change I *don't* choose that catches me off guard and has been the most difficult to embrace.

Through deep reflection and hard work I've learned to accept change and see it as an opportunity to learn and grow. I don't love it, but at least I know that something good will accompany any discomfort that it brings. I've learned to be strong and mindful of the next opportunity change will bring.

As a mature adult I now treat change like a hiccup, and you can too. Here's my prescription for dealing with change:

1. Be shocked at the change, particularly when it's a big one.
2. Cry and scream and kick.
3. Seek comfort from an appropriate source:
   - friend, therapist, spouse
   - but *not* from food, drink or someone who can't give you what you need. This includes people who are likely to say "Don't whine. It isn't that bad."
4. Stay in your comfort zone for a bit, either alone or with someone you trust, until you are distracted by something else, or you have to pee.
5. Don't fixate on what the change took from you, but focus on the good that will come from it. As one door closes, another one opens. You can't make room for the new until you let go of the old.

You may be saying, "Well, that sounds hunky dory, but she can't possibly be talking about such a dramatic change as the loss of a friend or loved one." But I am. When my spouse passed away two years ago I was a wreck. I cried myself sick. But from the beginning of this devastating loss I vowed to remain open and present. I knew that if I didn't walk through the process with awareness and openness, I'd still be crying a year later. There were some things I probably should have done differently in handling this grief. However, there is no perfection in how we respond to loss and change. I wanted to feel the loss, experience all the changes that came with it, and celebrate my relationship with him. I feel I did pretty well for myself and for honoring his memory and all the wonderful ways he was. I still miss him and can get teary-eyed, but at the same time I acknowledge that goodness has continued to flow through my life since his passing.

Change isn't meant to be easy. If you don't deal with it as it arises, it'll only get more difficult and destructive as time goes by. How you choose to deal with change is up to you.

Are you the dog that can learn new tricks regardless of how old you are, or are you so deeply rooted that when change does come, it knocks you on your butt?

Spring Ahead or Fall Back

Are you one of those people whose life becomes completely discombobulated because of Daylight Saving Time? One hour either way might not seem like much, but I have friends who are off-kilter for weeks after this one hour either magically appears or is abruptly taken away.

Daylight Saving Time (DST) decreases the amount of daylight in the morning hours, allowing for more daylight to be available during the evening. It was first proposed by entomologist George Vernon Hudson, whose shift-work job gave him leisure time to collect insects and led him to value after-hours daylight. He presented a paper in 1895 where he cited statistics proving that a one-hour change in time, causing people to rise earlier and use morning sunlight, significantly conserved candles and heating coal.

Winston Churchill took the DST ball and ran with it in England, saying it enlarged "the opportunities for the pursuit of health and happiness among the millions of people who live in this country." People who worked in agriculture and those in the evening entertainment business dubbed it "Daylight *Slaving* Time." The United States adopted DST in the early 20th century in order to conserve coal during wartime, along with Britain and Germany's allies in World War I.

You might be surprised to know that U.S. states are not federally mandated to observe daylight saving time. The only law that does exist stipulates that all states implementing DST observe it at the same time—from the second Sunday in March to the first Sunday in November. Prior to 2007 it was in effect from the first Sunday in April to the last Sunday in October.

DST continues to be controversial today. It doesn't

benefit farmers and others who rise before dawn and have to spend more time working before daybreak. But its benefits include saving energy and decreasing traffic accidents and incidents of crime.

One kink in DST is that not everyone observes it uniformly. Residents of Arizona and Hawaii, along with the US territories of Puerto Rico and the Virgin Islands, do not acknowledge Daylight Saving Time, but their lack of participation has been manageable over the years.

Most people make the transition more smoothly during the time change in autumn, when we get additional snooze time. But the sudden darkness even before the evening commute can take some adjustment. The spring change, however, while taking away that precious hour, allows us more time to frolic or laze in the warm afternoons.

Another more subtle change seems to accompany DST, and that is a certain feeling in the air. This feeling doesn't arrive on the exact hour given or taken away, but usually during some point within that week. In the spring, it feels a tad warmer in the morning when I take the garbage out, and I notice all the tiny blossoms beginning to bud. In the fall, there is a fleeting crispness in the air that makes me think about digging up the stored sweaters in preparation for cooler mornings ahead.

Daylight Saving Time signifies change, one I'm willing to embrace. It signals approaching holidays in the fall or a new warmth penetrating my bones in the spring. It's a life cycle that brings change yet remains unchanged from year to year.

One hour more or one hour less is not much when compared to the early Romans, whose daily clocks were tied to the rotation of the sun, which changed throughout the year. Some days had more minutes than others, and they varied from month to month. We should be grateful we only have to deal with two hours in the entire year, though it's easy for me to say since I'm not one of those bothered by the time change.

Does DST throw your sleep patterns out of whack? Are you cranky or spaced out when the time change occurs? Whatever your answer, don't forget to spring forward or fall back an hour when the time change comes!

Smile

Humor and laughter are powerful, but I frequently forget about the gifts they bring to my daily life by the way that they smooth out the ruffles of stress and tension.

In addition to reliving stress, several studies support the notion that laughter:

- relaxes the entire body;
- reduces levels of cortisol, thus minimizing pain and inflammation throughout the body;
- releases endorphins, those natural, feel-good substances that make you feel happy and content;

- reduces blood pressure and improves blood circulation and oxygen intake.

That's the medical point of view. These are all good things for anybody but particularly for seniors who seek diverse ways to improve their health. The fun part of the equation, though, is something I never remember often enough.

I've been to comedy shows where my sides have literally ached the next day from laughing so hard, and I always swear I'll go to those shows on a more regular basis. It's just plain fun. Being in a happy place melts my woes away. You can't focus on the negative when you're laughing.

There's no excuse for not letting the power of humor and laughter lift you to new heights of happiness and well-being.

6½ Ways to a Contented Life

1. Ask for help.

Life is too short to waste time trying to do it all on your own. If there is someone who can help, ask them. My husband and I recently wanted to barbecue, but neither of us knew how. We didn't want to flounder around on our own, so we asked a friend who barbecues often for help, and now we're on our way to being expert outdoor cooks.

2. Simplify your life.

Simplifying your life can start with that spring cleaning you never quite get around to starting. You probably have many objects in your home that you never use. These things clutter up both physical and mental space that could be available for exciting, new experiences and people.

3. Focus on the positive.

My pet peeve is wasting time in conversation about negative things beyond our control—the weather, nasty politics, celebrity gossip, wallowing in the bad experiences of others. This kind of talk doesn't help anybody. It only wastes time and keeps your life from being better.

4. Meditate.

Meditation relaxes the way your mind processes some of the crazy situations in life. A regular practice of meditation alleviates much of the "monkey mind" of energetic discourse that overwhelms us despite our best efforts to not let things get to us.

5. Look for what's important.

If the end of the world was near, what would you spend your last days doing, and with whom? Would you want it to be about family and friends, or getting even with someone, or buying an expensive car or house or outfit?

6½. Share your wealth.

I give this one an extra half because not only does it help others, it helps you at least half as much more than it helps them. When everything in my life suddenly looks like a disaster, the best thing I can do for myself is to do something good for someone else. This takes the focus off me and my problem, and benefits someone else. Some of the most powerful giving I have done in my life has come when I turn away from an inane issue in my life to help another.

That Half-Full Glass

Whatever you put in your glass is what it will be filled with. That's pretty obvious. However, what I really mean is that whatever we bring into our lives, whatever we spend time and money on, whatever receives the best of our attention and efforts, that will be what our lives are filled with.

If the glass is only half full, that means there's a lot more you could be doing to enrich your life and have it be more fulfilling. If it's full but murky with goop, that means it needs to be emptied and then refilled with the good stuff. If the glass is filled with crystal clear water, but it gradually turns grey, that means it's time to find what is seeping into your water and get rid of it.

This example illustrates just how much of our happiness is within our control. When we look outside ourselves and see the economy, the weather, our friends, family or neighbors behaving badly, when we can't get beyond our body shape and size or the wrinkles on our faces, we can easily sink into frustration and not want to do anything to make life better.

The truth is you have the power to make life sweet and satisfying and fun and rewarding and silly and memorable all by yourself. Nothing is needed; you can do this without money, without a job or a fancy home, without all the answers to the millions of questions you are plagued with daily. There's a patch of fresh green grass with your name written on it, and it is up to you to step into that space and claim it for yourself. But how can you achieve it?

You want the glass filled with crystal clear water, but what must you do to get it?

The way to get what you want is to make room for it. Get out of your own way and make the necessary space for the good stuff to enter. Your glass may need to be emptied and refilled, or the contents added to or enhanced with more clean water.

A technique I use is to remind myself that my time on this earth is limited. What am I going to spend my time on today if I only have a small amount of time left? I know it's not going to matter what I look like or how the stock market performed.

On the day I was diagnosed with breast cancer, twenty-two years ago, I felt my life implode. I was told my time on Earth was much shorter than I originally planned. However, I did receive one wonderful gift from that experience: an instantaneous recognition of what is important and where I wanted to spend my remaining time. I wanted to be with my family and friends, with my cat, my books, and a nice glass of chardonnay. In an instant, my life moved from being murky with goop to crystal clear with meaning and joy.

Don't let a serious illness—or anything else—rob you of your glass of water, however you want it to look. Time is limited. Take control of your happiness today!

My Dad

My dad was a difficult man to love. He was an alcoholic, verbally abusive, and madly in love with my mother, who kept him tethered on a tenuous lead. I was afraid of him and I loved him. As an older adult I can now admire all that he overcame to make a wonderful life for his family, of which I'm the only remaining member.

He was born on a farm in Milwaukee, the son of Polish/Italian parents. His father, Nick Albany, died at the age of twenty-four of rheumatic fever. His mother remarried and provided a stable yet meager home for him and his sister.

Dad began his career in show business. He was in Ziegfeld Follies and became "The Human Echo." He'd simultaneously parrot back to you what you were saying to him, whether you were speaking English or any other language. This talent of his used to annoy the hell out of me because he'd echo me whenever I was upset. I felt he was mocking me, but I see now he was just trying to add some levity to my immature angst.

Once he was married and there were little ones to consider, he joined the Army Air Corps, which later became the Air Force. This career allowed us to travel all over the world, and we lived in Japan and France. As a youngster, I wasn't thrilled about being away from cool American stuff when I lived in foreign countries, but today I see that my broad outlook of the world is based on these foreign living experiences, for which I am now immensely grateful.

Dad died thirty-eight years ago, and I miss him. He was sometimes a pain, especially when he'd make a pass at one of my girlfriends, but I am grateful for all that he did for us. He wanted the best for us and took pride in being able to give us something special in life. His trouble was with my mother; my sister and I just got caught in the middle, as so often happens to kids.

These days I think of him fondly, forgive all his foibles, and wish he was here to see how well I've done under his early tutelage.

Celebrating Freedom, Senior Style

As we age, our sense of freedom and its implications become heightened. Perhaps this is because our lives are not as splintered with family and work obligations or a boatload of other duties. The simplicity of my later years has allowed me to focus on the basics of life, and freedom is right up there at the top of my most-important-things-in-life list.

I never wait until July Fourth to celebrate freedom and what it means to me. I celebrate it every day that I am able to move through my community without fear of sniper attacks or bombings. I know there will always be aberrations, such as the shootings at Newton or Columbine, but generally speaking I feel safe in my community compared to people living in war-torn parts of the world.

I celebrate freedom every time I acquire the book of my choice from a library or bookstore, or freely leave the U.S. for foreign travel, or attend the spiritual home of my choice for prayers and learning, all without the involvement or questioning by others. These are some of the things not afforded to everyone in the world, and I don't take them for granted.

My freedom includes spending my time and money and energy on people and activities of my choosing. Though taxes and death will always be around whether I choose them or not, my life is one filled with the choices I make.

I am grateful beyond words for the freedom I have, and am eternally grateful for those people who fought to ensure my freedom.

"Get Over It" Packs a Punch!

When something goes wrong, get over it.

When disappointment barges in, get over it.

When emotional hurt becomes a burden upon your spirit, get over it.

The bitterness from these situations will take root and hold problems in your subconscious unless you get over them.

Do you want to know what holding on to grief, anger, stress, anxiety and general negativity actually does? It kills you, physically, emotionally and spiritually. That may sound harsh, but I believe it is true. I can feel the life being sucked out of me when I've clung to something negative for longer than its expiration date.

Getting over it means releasing the negative power from a situation or person. Getting over it means moving on to the next fun, creative, challenging, inspiring, motivating, uplifting and joyous thing life has just for you.

I love how we learn from our pets. I never see Kali, my beloved kitty, hang on to terror, as she could have when a plastic bag stuck to her one good back leg and chased her frantically around the house, or disappointment, like when I tell her, "No snacks right now, missy." I can recall more than once when I've come waltzing around the corner only to smash into her precious, little face with my big foot. She darts off in pain and confusion but returns moments later, when I'm sitting down, for a love-fest petting session. I may be over-anthropomorphizing, but the point is she gets over it.

Despite their lack of higher education, our pets have a great deal to teach us.

So, the next time...

- someone cuts you off in traffic;
- someone forgets to do something you asked them;
- someone doesn't invite you to the party;
- someone hurts your feelings,
- you fail at something;
- you act harshly to yourself or others;
- you relapse into bad behavior...

...stop and do yourself a favor:

GET OVER IT!

And move on to goodness.

For the Love of Pets

Many of my friends talk about the emotional impact their pets have had on their lives, especially those friends who are now senior citizens. In most cases, the kids are gone, and, for some, their spouses have passed away. With boring TV and difficulty getting around or exploring too far from home, the days loom large. Pets who depend on us and love us in return can make a huge difference in the happiness of a senior's life.

I freely admit just how bananas I am about my precious cat, Kali. Never having had children or step-children to spend time with, I've transferred my maternal instincts onto my pets all throughout my adult life. I'm unashamedly guilty of anthropomorphizing and imbuing my pets with human feelings and emotional characteristics.

I am not alone in this. Go to any dog park and you can see the pride that owners have for their animals. They are proud of how their Sparky or Bessie stays close by while off leash or runs back and forth to check in with their owners. You can see the love and admiration in their faces as Toby or Cosmo checks out other dogs with a friendly perked-up tail.

When for some reason our animals disappoint us, like shredding the toilet paper roll or tearing up the corner of a kitchen cabinet during the frenzied noise of July Fourth fireworks, we manage to forgive them quickly. We know their behavior was due to boredom or fear and not meant to hurt or anger us.

I love my cat Kali unconditionally, without question. I know that she is connected to me as the main human in her life, and in this way I'd like to think that she loves me back. Since Kali spends so much of her time showing devotion to me, it makes sense that I want to show her that same devotion in return.

I wish I could love every human being the easy way I love Kali. I wish I could suspend all other motives and emotions and love everyone purely, without question, all the time. I wish I didn't get enraged sometimes or hurt by the actions of other people.

In spite of my lack of perfection in the human love department, I can learn from Kali. She can teach me to love others the way she loves me. I am made better by her love.

What If?

What would it be like if for one entire day you allowed only goodness into your life? What if, during that 24-hour period, you viewed every single situation, thought, conversation and action as something positive?

What if the next time you are cut off in traffic you give thanks that there was no accident or that you were not delayed? What if the next time you *are* delayed, you acknowledged it as a reminder to make more time for future travel or to slow down in general?

What if you didn't take it personally the next time a friend, family member or co-worker, who was only thinking they were being funny, made a snotty remark to you? What if, when you didn't meet your deadline, you acknowledged yourself for being diligent and trying hard, instead of kicking yourself and letting it ruin your day?

What if, for just one day, the goodness and abundance of life filled you to overflowing? How might your life be changed?

It's a choice: being upbeat about the circumstances in your life versus being crabby because you let things get to you. It's a choice you make a thousand times a day.

You may think, "That sounds good! How do I start?" You start anytime and anywhere. Start where you are right now; goodness will meet you there. Stay in gratitude for everything. Being in that place will change your perspective and uplift every outcome. A consciousness of all that is available to you will send multiples of goodness your way.

Stop complaining about your life, and make the most of all that you have. Stop comparing yourself to other people, who you think are happier just because they have more, do more, or appear more. Your own happiness won't come marching into your life unless you open the door and let it in.

What if you made a different choice, just for today, and met your joy in the process?

Getting an "F" in Retirement

I have failed to live up to the basic standards for retirement living.

A popular attitude these days tells us we should feel "less than" if we don't pursue something productive every day. However, doesn't the very definition of retirement include permission to enjoy the little things of nothingness or the luxury of a looming afternoon with no agenda?

Who sets these standards for us? "They" do, that's who. It's the proverbial "they" who set the rules for much of what we say, do, buy, feel and express.

Though I hate to admit it, I am often gullible enough to accept what "they" say. For example, I feel proud when someone says about me, "She's busier now than she ever was before retirement." I wear this comment like a badge of honor. It tells me I'm no goof off, no slacker retiree wasting time with no purpose.

When people ask how you are, do you respond quickly with a litany of all that you are doing in your busy weeks? A friend of mine would do this every time we met, so one time I repeated the question back to her more seriously, "Yeah, but how are you really doing?" She almost burst into tears. She hadn't previously slowed down long enough to feel much of anything.

Is your schedule always filled but your life seldom fulfilling? Perhaps you're buying into what "they" say we should be doing during retirement. To get a better handle on how my retirement is going, I regularly check in with the following seven benchmarks:

1. Do I wake with enthusiasm, eager to enjoy what the day has to offer?

2. Is there enough empty space on my calendar to

make room for some serious goof-off time?

3. Do I feel fulfilled with my friendships and family fellowship?

4. Do acquaintances feel I'm available for a spur-of-the-moment coffee date?

5. Do I spend the majority of my time talking about positive things in life rather than the aches and pains, the weather or the economy?

6. Do I feel I'm living my life based on what I want to do rather than what others expect me to be doing?

7. At the end of the day, do I feel okay about myself even if I don't have something tangible to show for my day, like piles of clean laundry, pages of written text or a garden free of weeds?

If I can answer "yes" to a majority of these, I'm on the right track in my retirement. Don't get me wrong, though. I can feel like a real slug that has nothing to show for my time if I spend the entire day reading, even if it's for research. I'm not always doing the best at my retirement, but I keep trying to keep things in balance.

The best way to determine if you're doing retirement right is to ask yourself if you are living a meaningful life. If the answer is "yes," that's all we can ask for. Like everything else, it's a process.

On Being Human

Oh, how I wish I could get it right. How I wish I could just wake up one morning and not do anything to hurt another person or frustrate them or make them roll their eyes. Have you ever wished this? It's like waking up on the morning of a new diet. "Today I'm going to get it!" But I'm not talking about dieting. I'm talking about containing, managing and corralling my human side.

My spiritual side is always perfect, whole, open, just the way it is. My human side, on the other hand, speaks without listening and, in an effort to be cute or knowledgeable or correct, says hurtful things to others. Why?

Why am I not able to just keep my mouth shut? Why can't I let another person say and feel and do what they want, even if I know a better way or if I disagree with their process? I'm pretty smart. You'd think I'd know to just listen.

Intellectually I know that my spiritual and human sides are one, that my angst about being imperfect is just where I'm supposed to be. Knowing this, however, doesn't raise me up, at least not today. I want to stop saying and doing hurtful things. I want to be that person that others emulate, that person people want to be with because they can know that I'm not going to be a jerk.

Does this sound like a pity party? Perhaps so. Maybe you've been where I am. I know that as we evolve and grow, moments like this feel harsh and like a million steps backward. It's all part of the process of being human.

Ten Lessons on Enlightenment

It's powerful to get a glimpse of how majestically simple life can be. These ten spiritual life lessons have, over the years, helped me embrace this simplicity:

1. We are all one. Caring for and honoring others is caring for and honoring ourselves.

2. Life's most valuable lessons, like unconditional love and lack of ego, can be learned from our pets. Observe your pets closely, and you will see this is true. If they stumble and fall or if you ignore their at-

tempts to garner affection, they don't walk away embarrassed and miffed. They just move on to the next thing in life.

3. Get in touch with yourself and listen to your inner dialogue. The reasons we're feeling a certain way can be found inside ourselves, not in the people or things that surround us.

4. Learning to truly forgive yourself and others will set you free.

5. The value of friendship far outweighs material wealth.

6. To honestly listen with patience and interest to someone else is one of your greatest and most appreciated skills.

7. Good health is a precious possession. Treat yourself accordingly.

8. Letting go of expectations will allow you to receive life's greatest gifts. You can't grab the good if your hands are tied up with what you think you /should/ be getting.

9. No one controls you; you are free to be and do all that is possible. Don't squander your talents.

10. Invite others to join your path to happiness by being a joyous person that others want to spend time with. A negative attitude is mentally and physically exhausting and is off-putting.

This is my set of lessons that have proven effective in moving my life forward in a simple and loving way. What are yours?

Time Running Out

Time is more valuable than money. You can always make more money, but you can't make more time. Time goes by whether you're doing something productive or just sitting on your ass. It marches on whether you're listening to a sermon or reality TV.

Time can't be bundled up and stored in safekeeping for future use. It's here now and then it's gone. Today is today; it isn't coming back.

The best way to honor your time is to use it wisely. Today and every day is a gift to be experienced with joy and passion. Life as a whole is a gift to be lived with joy and passion. At bedtime, can you reflect on the day and feel you have honored it? Or have you succumbed to hours of mindless television or gossip or negative people?

How much of your time is unfocused, unmotivated or unplanned? It is a good idea to assess how much time you spend online, planning meals, reading the news, missing or being late for appointments, commuting, gossiping, or arguing. How much time have you wasted being upset and angry? And for what? Taking a small amount of time to plan your day will help you avoid the many pitfalls of wasting time.

As with many retired seniors, I have more free time these days than when I worked. But that is no excuse to waste time. It's still important to have goals about the day or week ahead. Living with purpose is more productive and rewarding than not.

On the other hand, I'm a big fan of relaxing and smelling the roses, of resting and rejuvenating and re-fueling. Sometimes I have to schedule down-time to make sure it happens. Since we're both retired, my husband and I try to claim one day a week when we don't schedule appointments or chores.

When I hang out with people who consistently bring me down, I'm dishonoring the value of time. Many of us don't know how to extricate ourselves from people or conversations that solve no problems and serve no purpose other than to waste precious moments. Life is too short to be in the presence of people who are chronically negative. Doing so is sure to turn us into negative and cranky people as well. I'm not saying these are bad people, but just be aware of the power of their negativity and how it affects you.

I've been guilty of wasting large amounts of time trying to resolve tiny conflicts or respond to my every critic. It's not a good use of time to spin your wheels trying to convince everyone to like you. Some people never will. In recent years I've chosen the people closest to me by their positive attitudes and approach to life. My inner circle needs to reflect the enthusiastic and upbeat person that I am.

What did you do with your day today? Did you treat your time like valuable cash?

Judgment Can Be a Thief

I was reminded recently how bad it feels to be unfairly judged. I did something differently than a friend thought I should have done it. I didn't do a bad thing, and my choice in no way affected her. She just didn't have all the pertinent information as to why I decided to do what I did, and she didn't like it.

Our "differences among friends" might have been okay, except instead of reaching out to me and telling me how she felt, she simply withdrew and stayed away. For a couple of years! She withdrew even when I tried to communicate with her by asking if something was wrong and why she hadn't responded to my efforts to contact her.

What matters to me in this situation is that I'm thankful it happened. I'm thankful I got a firsthand lesson in exactly how awful it feels to be judged for my actions. It is a huge reminder not to judge what others may say or do, but to remember that there's much more going on in their lives than I will ever know.

When I don't understand the actions of another person, it's probably better to simply stand by and continue to be the good friend that I am, silently.

Judging can be a good thing. We need to judge situations and people to make sure they are not harmful and injurious to our hearts, bodies or souls. However, judging or misjudging the actions, attitudes and beliefs of others robs people of their humanness. Misguided judgments we make about others can steal our grace by lessening the unconditional love we feel for others.

Because we are required to make judgment calls on so many aspects of everyday life, it's easy to misjudge someone else's judgment calls. One of the traps of judging is that it usually stops any further communication.

If we arrive at a negative judgment, we don't usually pursue the situation or person further to find out if we were correct in our assumptions, which we probably shouldn't have made in the first place.

In the future, before making a judgment, I will:

- Listen to what is said with an open mind;
- Ask a ton of probing questions;
- See if my opinion and attitudes get in the way of seeing the clear picture;
- Ask myself if it matters. Does their behavior or decision affect me at all?
- Convey my final decision to pull away or be upset in a clear and timely manner.

I miss my friend and I forgive her. I wish we hadn't wasted these years on a judgment that went off the rails.

Be Here Now

Have you ever spent days ruminating over something you did in the past or on a decision you made that can't be changed? Have you ever noticed yourself so focused on something in the future that when you get home, you don't remember driving your car there? The "now" in both of these examples is merely a fleeting concept, yet being in the now is the richest, most delicious place to hang out.

When I'm inside, I wish I was outside, and when I'm outside I'm sure there's something I should be doing inside. At these times, the now is nowhere in sight. It is challenging to be in the now when I'm worried or in pain or stressed. However, this is the best time to practice being still and calm and centered on what is right in front of me.

My "monkey mind"—that incessant chatter that rolls around in your head—sometimes keeps me from focusing on being calm. I have struggled with this when I meditate and when I attempt to focus on what's going on in the moment. Though the monkey mind isn't the enemy, it only gets louder if I treat it as such. If I respond to it more like an insolent child, shushing it with compassion and love, it immediately begins to quiet.

When my spouse passed, I promised myself to stay in the moment and feel the entirety of the grief experience. I let go of doing and saying the appropriate thing. I let go of not taking time for myself when I needed it. I let go of comforting others and of eating this and not eating that. I can say today that my grieving process progressed much smoother than it could have because I did it my way. I let the feelings of pain come in and didn't try to avoid, cover or postpone them. My feelings and actions didn't match what others might have expected, but I stayed in the now throughout the difficult experience.

What's the advantage of being in the now? Doesn't it benefit us to assess situations by using the past to help us learn what to do in the future? Doesn't it help us prevent mistakes if we analyze the past? Yes and no.

In order to avoid past mistakes, we do need to take stock of prior experiences and plan for the future. To obsess with everything that went wrong in the past or could go wrong in the future is where we begin wasting time. This obsession serves no purpose except to detract from the joy of right now.

What is in front of you now to enjoy and appreciate? Is there anything from the past or the future that might be clouding that lovely and exciting look at the now?

Painfully Yours

What does physical pain do to your overall well-being? When I stub my toe, I jump around and moan for about twenty seconds, and then the pain begins to subside. But what about pain that lasts and lasts? There are many people, some of them senior citizens, who live with pain every day of their lives.

One day I received a new partial at the dentist to replace an old one. The minute I popped it in my mouth, it clamped around the two anchoring teeth with a vengeance and I knew it wasn't going to be coming out anytime soon. Sure enough, it stuck and soon began digging into my gum. I was in severe pain for the next twenty-four hours until I was able to see the dentist.

This experience made me wonder what chronic pain must be like, especially for older people. It made me feel somewhat indignant. Why in this day and age does pain have to exist even for a short period of time? I tried being at one with the pain, but it seemed to be winning.

While I'm not a big pill popper, I would have welcomed a break from the pain, even if it was just temporary. Excedrin finally allowed me to sleep without as much pain, but what about people for whom a pill isn't the answer? How do others learn to live with pain?

People with chronic pain have my admiration. The things currently at their disposal are: biofeedback, chronic pain management clinicians, meditation, breathing exercises, increasing endorphins through physical movement and support groups, none of which provide a quick solution.

A friend of mine has had a pretty bad headache for a couple of years now. She's sought medical help from many doctors, had hundreds of tests and even was evaluated in the hospital with various possible remedies. I think I'd be pretty cranky if I had to live with this discomfort for very long.

Perhaps there will come a time in my life when chronic arthritis or some other condition will force me to cope with an uncomfortable day-to-day level of pain.

I salute those who chronically suffer. I can't imagine how they cope. If you're reading this and aren't in pain, be grateful. By the way, my dentist did finally get the partial out, but I made him shoot me full of Novocain first.

A Labyrinth to Longevity

Who is the oldest person you know? What are they like? Are they cranky like Scrooge or upbeat, active and optimistic? You don't have to live a perfect life to live a long life, but I believe your attitudes, beliefs, moods and overall personality have a powerful impact on longevity.

We all know people who seem excessively younger or older than their chronological years. Do their moods and personalities differ from those of other people? If you've been overweight or a persistent smoker or been stressed most of your life, your longevity will be affected as you age. Several studies going back to the 1920s show that other non-lifestyle factors may significantly affect how long some people live. With this in mind, the following four traits can lengthen the lives of older people.

1. Socialization

Spending time with people in relationships that include positive emotions, loving feelings, stimulating interactions can reduce stress, inflammation and cardiovascular disease. Belonging to a book club or meeting friends for lunch or to play cards, for instance, brings meaning into our lives, especially after retirement.

2. Optimism

Most research finds that people who live longer approach life optimistically and don't sweat the small stuff. There are studies, however, that say some who look at everything overly optimistically may disregard the impact of the evils of excess, like drinking and smoking, and a shunning of medications and proper exercise.

3. Volunteer Work/Selfless Service

While I automatically assume that volunteer work would be good for the mind, body and spirit, I heard from one source that it's the motivation for volunteering that dictates whether your volunteer work helping others will increase longevity or not. Evidently, longevity is not enhanced if your volunteer work is for self-oriented reasons such as boosting your own ego or for gaining work experience.

4. Being Open

Being open to new experiences helps us handle change and adapt to challenging problems. However, being open isn't easy to quantify; it's very subjective. When I'm open, I'm not as dependent on the opinions of others and I don't stress as much about "doing it the right way."

There are many paths that lead us to the same goal. What are yours? Even if you don't agree that these things increase longevity, at the very least they make for a more pleasant experience while we're among the living.

Should You or Shouldn't You?

Should is one word that should be eliminated from our vocabulary. Oops, guess it isn't so easy to do! Every time I hear *should*, I cringe. My experience has been that *should* is usually accompanied by some standard established by "them," those faceless people we allow to run our lives.

What is this *should* and where did it come from? My guess is it came from our childhood, from both home and school. And now we continue incorporating it into our adult lives. We effortlessly continue setting myriad standards based on these *shoulds*.

"Should" is the simple past tense of the word *shall*, but these two words seem far apart. "I shall do something" sounds so purposeful and elegant, while "I should do something" sounds slightly angry and parental.

It's time to let go of *should*. Regardless of where *should* came from, it's time to unwind the habit of using it to communicate our knowledge, opinions, wants, and better judgments.

Don't waste everyone's time by verbalizing what you know is best but is clearly something you don't want to do. As far as other people are concerned, never say what someone else should or shouldn't do. If the "shh" sound begins to escape your lips, immediately stop yourself. No one wants you to be their conscious or better judgment; leave that to them. They either will or won't.

I rarely make any lasting changes from a negative stance. Thus, to wave a *should* in front of me is a guarantee that I won't do it. When I'm kind and compassionate with my less-than-glowing behavior, thoughts or words, I feel a slight shift toward the positive, which is better than none. I may, for entertainment, read that list on the Internet of ten foods I shouldn't eat, but that's all it is to me: a suggestion prepared by "them." And, as we all know, you shouldn't listen to them.

How Skeptical Do You Need to Be?

Though I believe in the innate kindness of human beings, and though I trust others have my best interests at heart, this is not always the case.

I've been noticing how much fraud is being reported these day and that senior citizens are the targeted market for these scams more often than most other groups. While I want to believe and trust those who approach me, my friends and I are finding ourselves closing the door on offers that sound awfully tempting.

I've been taught to be polite, to hear someone out, and certainly not to slam the door in their faces. Yet I

The Other Side of the Hill

find myself having to do this more and more to keep myself protected from scams and rip-offs.

The reasons seniors are targeted more than other age groups are:

1. Seniors tend to have larger savings accounts;
2. Those of us born in the 1930s, 40s and 50s were raised to be polite and trusting;
3. Elderly Americans are less likely to report fraud because they're embarrassed or because they don't know who they should report it to;
4. Senior citizens are more susceptible to products that will aid their health and provide more comfort and ease.

I could provide a complete treatise on all the different kinds of scams directed at seniors and what to do to avoid them. Suffice it to say, beware. If it looks too good to be true, it is. Don't sign anything that you don't completely understand, and don't hesitate to say you want to wait for a friend or family member to participate in the decision.

What can you do to balance a healthy sense of skepticism with a desire to trust and believe? This is a difficult question to answer. One thing that generally works for me is to ask my friends for their input before deciding to purchase or not. I ask them, "Do you know about this or that?" "What do you think about it, and what was your experience working with the sellers?" Even with these questions, though, there is no guarantee you'll escape being a victim someday.

I dislike letting suspicion get in the way of being open to the goodness of the Universe. I try to remain open to the joys of every day and trust that my simple life is good just as it is, without those products or services that promise much but in actuality deliver little in making life more productive or fun.

My Crystal Ball

Oh, how I'd love to have a crystal ball. I'd love to know how it all ends. I'd love to know why I should not wait to write that e-mail or make a long postponed phone call. I'd love to know whether I should hurry or slow down with the next book, either in the reading or writing of it.

Am I destined to live alone in the years ahead? Will I be discarding my things and moving into a smaller place at some point? As a woman without children or other family-of-origin members still living, I wonder what my future living situation will be.

When I worked on the 2010 U.S. Census, I surveyed group homes in our city and took a long look to see if I could visualize myself residing in one of those places. The homes, which typically housed six to eight seniors, were comfortable and inviting. The residents, however, seemed somewhat at sea. They were confined to wheelchairs or lying in bed; no one was reading or having a conversation. While this part of what I saw didn't look very inviting, I tried not to project my mindset on them. Those people may very well have been quite content with their lives, even though I think I would not.

For those of us who are more active and mentally curious, the issue of isolation is a question. Without knowing what my future needs will be, I feel it is my job to plan for any eventuality. Because I'm a proactive person, I want to be prepared. But how? I'm not sure how to begin planning for my future living arrangements.

How do I look to life in the future and still stay firmly rooted in my life today? When I look to what might be, I feel curious at best and worried at worst. Thank goodness for a strong mindfulness practice that keeps me grounded in today.

Living with an intense focus on the present and a curious look to the future will serve me best. I will continue to read articles about what other senior citizens are doing to live most comfortably in their remaining years. However, it will be with a sense of curiosity and not angst or commitment that I will absorb the information.

Since I can't control the future, releasing the fear of what my living arrangements might be is my best strategy. But I won't let this conversation dictate my actions today. Today is for enjoying where I live right now.

ANTONIA ALBANY has written about aging issues for several years in blog posts and her latest book entitled *Golden Grace: Embracing the Richness of Our Later Years*. She shares her humorous, spiritual and practical views on making the most of our senior years in this book and at her website, TheJoyOfAgingGratefully.com.

She lives in the wine country of northern California with her husband and cat and is available for public speaking engagements.